AF440955

Watch Yourself

By

Downtown Pat Brown

Copyright @ 2020 by Downtown Pat Brown, All Rights Reserved

The views expressed in this work are solely those of the author. Names, characters, places and incidents are the product of the author's. Any resemblance to actual persons, living or dead, events or locales is entirely for the purpose of the author's autobiographical memory only.

No part of this publication may be reproduced, distributed or transmitted without the express consent and written permission of the publisher.

Creative Direction: Patricia E. Brown, Tamiko Lowry-Pugh, Patricia Dallas

Publisher: Still Standing Publishing Company

Edited by: Brown & Taylor Associates Literary Services

Photographs: Courtesy of Patricia E. Brown

Printed in the United States of America

ISBN: 9798703362211

Acknowledgements

To My TRIBE... Which is what my *Dad* use to say...

"*Who Tribe You Belong To?*"

To all of you... My Tribe

My Children, grandchildren, great grandchildren

And great great grandchildren... So glad, I was able to live to see it!

Two things in life, you must do to survive...

"PAY ATTENTION" and "WATCH YOURSELF"

Dedication

This book is dedicated to my siblings

Gwendolyn, Arlene and Joseph

And to my Oldest Living Aunt

Gladys Speed Maul

In Memoriam

My Two Oldest Children

Kenneth Victor Brown

Dec. 31, 1952 – Nov. 23, 2009

∞ ∞ ∞ ∞

Cynthia Renee Land Lewis

Aug. 22, 1957 – Feb. 9, 2015

∞ ∞ ∞ ∞

CONTENTS

Introduction

Ash Wednesday 2020

I went across the hall to check on my sick neighbor; meanwhile, some of my other neighbors had started looking for me. They know every now and then, they'd see me roaming the hall, to the 2nd floor laundry room, incinerator or to the Community Room (Yes, the same Community Room, where my first book, "*Pay Attention*" signing and launch was to take place, but due to the onset of the "*Coronavirus*," it had to be cancelled) and the rest is history. So, being the Comedian "*Mom's Mabley*," prototype that I am... I took advantage of the time that I have left on this side... to give you some more of "*Me.*" I never thought, at 80 years old, I'd write a book, let alone a second one. But I am so happy to join my *offspring's* to have become a published Author!

Nevertheless, my neighbor walked towards my apartment door and said, "*We saw that your door was ajar,*" when they caught up with me, in the community room. I yelled back, "*You know, I'm around!*" (We constantly look out for one another, because we're up in age, and we could, at any time, be in the hospital for one *thang* or another and I can't tell you how many of my neighbors have already gone on to glory, since I moved in... which has just been shy of two years, yet, I continued, "*I always leave it open, ain't nobody going in there!*" They just laughed, and said, "*Here she goes!*"

They know me... I had already been up and out "*early.*" I tell the other seniors, all the time, "*I don't sit around.*" They need to get out... Like I do! Well, anyway, I had gone to a pantry and set the extra goods, out on the "*free*" table, for them. You see, I had free slips to get things like milk, bread and other items and then announced, "*You gotta go get stuff... aint nothin' gonna come to you!*"

So, now that I'm back in the house, and got my lottery numbers in, at "*Mandela's Market,*" for the next 3 to 4 days; I ain't worried about going back outside today, *though I wish I could.* You see, I won't be able to get my "*Ashes*" today, but that's alright *the Lord knows I'm here...* 'cuz I'll go outside and get some dirt and put that on my forehead and make a cross myself right across my forehead! I remember a few other times, too, when I *wasn't* able to go get my *Ashes*; because I was sick or in the hospital.

So, I went out and mingled with the neighbors, pre-selling my book "*Pay Attention.*" They assured me that they were indeed going to buy it (and might I add, that by the time of publication... they stuck to their word, as many of you and purchased it). *THANK YOU!*

I was serious about my book too; you couldn't get a sneak peak, unless you were buying it.

You see, *"there's more than one way to skin a cat."* Coronavirus, didn't stop nuttin', but a formal reception but as I told my old fogies, *"y'all wasn't worried about catching nothing, back in the day... when ya was lickin' every thang all up and down, so don't be scared now"... All any of you can do, from here on out, is just... "WATCH YOURSELF!"*

By Downtown Pat Brown

Get On Up

I'm
still
getting around
while
you
still
Sitting around

Stay Ready

I stay ready... to keep from gettin' ready! I never drove; so I established a pattern of being ready for my ride, a long time ago. If someone say, they coming to get me... I'm ready at the door, with my bags packed. And if it's a Casino trip, my luggage, ready too! And if nobody come get me, bet yo' bottom dolla'... I'll beat you to where I got to go and you drivin'. And that's on 2 to 3 buses. Back in the day, we had transfers and tokens, to deal with. Now, all I have to do, is carry my senior transportation badge around my neck, for a discount and a small fare. Oh, and don't give me a *time*... I'm really ready! Because like I say, *I don't sit around.* I be out. I don't wait around for nobody... never have. My kids be calling me, I be all out at the Credit Union, the University Plaza on the train, or the Casino.

Humpf! This brings me into the story to tell you, how after my oldest sister and bruh-in-law made their way back to Toledo, after decades of relocating back to Buffalo and wah-la, just like that… I've visited her twice this summer during '*Corona*,' once in July and there again, in August; more than I've ever visited her when she lived only twenty minutes away. In Buffalo, I'd probably just see her once a year on her birthday. Shame, family leave, then we visit, but my point is, when one of my daughter's said, you want to go see your sister and check on her (*because she was in the hospital*), I said, "*Come get me! My bags already at the door!*" When we arrived at that hospital, it was all of these special visiting hours, I said, "*I'll turn dis blank blank out, I'm going to see my sister, up in here today, I came from out of town… I betcha dey let me in… I don't play… "WATCH YOURSELF!"*

Mickey D's

Some ole' geeser
in the building
tryna be slick
He wanna take
me to *McDonald's*
I don't want no
Mickey D's
take me to
T.G.I.F. Friday's

Um Drankin'

In 2009, I spoke with my Doctors, who thought it was necessary, that I have a bypass surgery on my left leg. This operation was to correct the blood circulation through my veins. I didn't tell my sons and my daughters til nearly time for the surgery, *like a few days away.* At this point, in time, I was 70 years old, *thinking* I was 50; trying to still make my own health decisions, but they weren't too happy, that they had not been, *fully* consulted. But, *a girl's gotta do… what a girl's gotta do…* especially, if I wanted to keep, "*droppin' it… like it's hot,*" (my most famous and favorite signature dance move of all time). Well anyway, I remember all of my adult children, rallying and praying around me as I was being rolled down the hall; then that moment, when *'none of your family can go any further came,'* and I waved *'see ya,'* as a *'goodbye,'* for now. Trying *not to* drop a tear. Hours later, it was a sure thrill, that I made it through surgery with flying colors and once I woke up in Recovery, I told my family, *"As I was coming 'back to' from under the anesthesia, all I could see was the big green gallon jug of "Carlo Rossi" wine… flying over my head."* And I followed it and woke up," I recalled telling them, by motioning with my neck, from one side to the other of how I was following that bottle. I'm here to tell ya' that a little wine ain't never *hurt* nobody. *"WATCH YOURSELF!"*

For Pete's Sake

It was Christmas day, 2014, December 25th... You know where to find me, baby... While everybody at their houses, opening up presents, drinking egg nog, cooking and spreading cheer... I was at my favorite spot. Yep, "*THE CASINO!*" Plus, you know *thangs* ain't like they used to be. People don't put up lights no mo' or nuttin'. I used to party; dress up with my Santa Claus suit and hat... *all dat!* Put up a tree, garnish it and don't forget the star at the top or the colorful strobe light underneath. *Those were the days!* Well, I do have a cell phone and at first it took a little getting used to; but I managed with my *Obama* phone and really love that they *up'd* the minutes, even though it doesn't seem to work in my building half the time. Nevertheless, it rang just as I was pressing '*cash out,*' to scoot over to another machine.   I answered, "*Yea-ah,*" like I normally do. It was one of my daughters, on the other end, asking me, '*where I was at,*' once I told her, she said, "*I'm coming to get you... I'll explain when I get there.*" So, I cashed out and mosied on with my rolling wheelchair towards the door to wait for her. Then, while on the way, driving over to my oldest daughter's house, that's when they told me... my Son-in-law, "*Pete,*" had died and they were waiting for... what we use to call, back in the day, '*the paddy wagon*' to come pick him up. By it being a holiday, we had to wait for the detectives, the coroner, the ambulance, *you name it.* So, it was getting tougher and longer by the minute; we were all trying to process this and we couldn't move him, so there he lay... there in the room... *and we wait... and we wait...* holding one another up. Finally, I said, "*I need to smoke a cigarette!*"   But, my daughter said that I would have to smoke outside. I said, "*Sh-i-i-i-t, y'all could have left me at the Casino, for all dis... when dey coming?!*" My daughter, Ann, (*and her kind husband*), who always take me... said ever so softly, "*You wanna us to take you back to the Casino, Ma?*" I replied, "*Hell, yea!*" "*WATCH YOURSELF!*"

I Don't Want Your Man

I don't want nuttin'
yella' (*yellow*)
Don't want nuttin'
lighter than me
I don't want your man
and I don't want *nan* now

Atlantic City

I almost lost my friend and client in the Atlantic ocean. Yep, I tried my hand at Home Health Care Aid too and took *'Big Jim,'* on my Atlantic City, New Jersey bus trip. We were on the Board Walk; me and my girlfriend/neighbor, *"Boog-a-loo,"* we were on one of those buggy's leaving Bally's and after a minute, I looked around and he was gone. He suffered from a little dementia, but I didn't know he was going to tip away. To back track a minute, I ended up taking him in, when my daughter, CoCo, was working up at Deaconess Hospital on Humboldt Parkway, *(another Landmark that's been torn down)*; she was making her rounds on one of the floors, this one particular shift and called me...

"Ma, guess who up here?"

I wondered, "*Who?*"

"*Big Jim,*" she said.

He was an ole' timer and family friend, then she added...

"*And he don't have nobody. You should take him in!*"

So, she found out how to have his check signed over to me and his residence changed to mine from the nursing facility, and soon he was released to my home for care. Fast forward, it was now time for the Casino Bus to leave, and lo and behold, I couldn't find him. Now, with a name like, 'Big Jim,' you have to know that he was quite a big fella, standing well over 6 feet tall and over no less than 200 pounds. So, needless to say, I missed the bus going back home and thank goodness, my one daughter lived outside of New York City, and came to my rescue. Now mind you, early '90's, we didn't have cell phones yet, but just so happen, I had written my daughter's telephone number down on a piece of paper, before I left home and put it in my purse. She drove to Atlantic City, New Jersey to help me find '*Big Jim*, but we couldn't. So, we made a police report and she drove me back home to Buffalo. Then, the call came in, a few days after from the authorities… They had found *Big Jim*, he was sitting up under the Pier, when the police found him and he was taken to the hospital, for hypothermia, and then my daughter and Cousin Teddy, (*my God-Sister Rose' son-in-law*) drove with my daughter Ann, to go back to get him to bring him back to Buffalo. Thank goodness, I didn't lose him. I was so relieved, and so was my family, whew! It wasn't until after his health worsened and he needed 24-hour care, that he had to be put into a nursing home. (Then, when he passed away, CoCo was right... he didn't have any family, my son *Main* and I were the only two that was at his memorial). No matter what, watch out for others and "*WATCH YOURSELF!*"

Catch Me If You Can

I always told
ya'll...
you have
to catch me
up early
in the morning,
before
I go 'pee'....

Long Island

Nope, not Long Island, NY... *Long Island Iced Tea*... You can make it yourself but once I saw it in the liquor store... I figured you can just buy it... and I been buying it every since. I buy a big gallon, of it, every time I go to the liguor store. You not a real drinker, if you buy small bottles, *naw naw*... you have to buy big bottles and buy more than one! Matter of fact, I still walk with my walker roller buggy up to *Bellamy's* up on East Ferry Street, and sho'nuff push it on back home; that along with my Vodka and Red Cat, (one of my grandaughter's introduced me to dat)! I was getting the name mixed up and was calling it *'Pussy Cat.'* (With my manish self. I laugh, to myself with the cracklin' sound, *'ah-kee-kee-kee'*). One day, I went outside, saw an empty liquor bottle that had been throwed on the ground and brought it in the house... bleached and wash it out, real good, and filled it up with Long Island. Yep, re-used it as a re-fill bottle. This was no ordinary empty bottle, it was from a very expensive liquor bottle... it had a cross on it, *that's probably what made me pick it up.* I did my Catholic hand cross blessing and kept it moving. You can do it now if you know how... *Do the hand motion, forming a letter "T"* tapping your forehead and chest and "*WATCH YOURSELF!*"

My Oldest

I raised him right, but the Service, I think did a *doozie* on him. He married a beautiful woman, (*true blue*) and we had the same first and last name, after they married and took on his last name. But *he* just couldn't get right. I gave them a nice wedding reception party and it broke my heart, that he messed up; hell, I drank too, but not like my boy. He drank so long, that I had to save his life, more than once. Guess he had it honest, it was definitely in our blood, *but you gotta know your limits.* I remember when I had to rush him to the hospital one day, and the doctors told me that I got him there right on time and that if he didn't stop drinking, we was going to lose him. Kenny had got *cirrhosis of the liver*, real bad. (*I remember not letting hm off the hook for his life insurance too, because I had paid for his life insurance a long while and said you paying now, because he was working again, but I would pay months up at a time, since I knew he would sometimes drink his payment up).* Well, *thank God,* she took the doctor's advice and stopped drinking for twenty years! He came clean... by then, he was divorced, went to *A.A.,* all dat. Received a lot of pins, awards and recognition, even got into church, which really revealed his kind character. We'd try to keep him up to date with his children and grandchildren, as he became a loner, for the most part. We'd see the family at my holiday parties, which were always so much fun. Back track, there was this one time, I found my oldest son fast asleep in my upstairs hallway, he had fortunately made it to my house and when I opened the door, there he was passed out on the floor...

I said, *"Boy what you doing and what's that in your hand?"*

"A sandwich," he said.

"Boy, why you still got it all balled up in your hand?"

"Well, you told me never to throw nuttin' away, Mama."

I started laughing so hard, *"Boy get up and get on in here and get sobered up!"* Sometimes, he reminded me more of like being my brother, since we were only 13 years apart. That's in, *'Pay Attention.'* But I loved him and he loved me. I even fed him til the day he died. I took chitterlings, turkey and dressing up to the hospital, all dat... every day, he had a meal. I didn't know what was happening when he started getting sick, now twenty years later; so, I moved him from his apartment building on West Utica to my street on Emerson Place, a few houses down and me and *Main, my baby boy*, would make sure he was alright. He was going back and forth to 'Veteran's' hospital. He started using the bathroom on himself, and I would cuss him out. I didn't know he was actually losing control of his organs, but again, I got him to the hospital, each time, but this one time, he didn't make it back home to us, the cirrhosis has re-surfaced and he didn't have long to live; then we got the call from the Staff, letting us know it was only going to be a matter of time... I didn't know how I was going to get through it, (*Thanks Sax!*). But, on the morning of November 23, 2009... I was throwin' dem *SHOTS back*... right at my bar... now I was ready to go bury my son. *"WATCH YOURSELF!"*

Attica

I remember my maternal grandmother, (*Mama*), used to take me, with her, to go see her son, there. I was only 3 years old and had a purple velvet outfit on. It was so beautiful. I don't know where she got it from. But I was always around *Mama,* (that's how I learned how to cook and clean). But anyway, her husband, *Papa* (my grandfather) was mad, pretty much all the time, that *Mama* would always keep sending him *curtains, sheets, food, money.... You name it...* to prison, saying, *"Once he get out... he's just going to go right back in!"* And *Papa* was right... my *Uncle Curt,* was in and out of prison from the time I was that *'little girl'*, until I was 60 years old. They called him the *drug kingpin,* (on the inside and out). Heroin was real bad back in the day. (As a teenager, I used to see him shooting up all dat... people coming to the house *to cop*). I even remember looking out of the window at our house on Bennett Street, to let my Uncle know when the police was coming. *"Here come the police!"* And they would raid the house; search it and everybody in the house, except me, because they could see that I was pregnant, but the drugs wasn't on me, anyway... Uncle would take the drugs and throw it up into the chandelier. Uncle had to even be escorted by police to his sister's funeral in 1971 (my mother), they brought him into Meadows Funeral Home, shackled at his feet and his arms, chained in front of him), they wouldn't let us touch him. If we tried, their arms went out to side to block us, "No touching!" All you could hear is, *"We love you brother and we love you Uncle"* throughout the Parlor. And the mourners were lined up from the corner end of Broadway Street all the way around the block to Jefferson Avenue to pay their respects, for my Mother. It was also, 1971, when the prisoners riot happened and seized control of Attica. We had no clue if

Uncle made it or not, or how he faired out, for a minute, until the inmates were accounted for. That was a nervous time for all of the families. But *HE HAD SURVIVED.* Then around about the late 1990's, my Uncle was *FINALLY* released, though he would pass away before he received any money from that whole upheaval, (God rest his soul, he passed peacefully, sitting on the couch, and was still in the same position, when my sister Bon Bon, made it to his apartment complex, even before the paramedics came). He actually lived in a building right behind Deaconness Hospital, both buildings are torn down now); but nevertheless, the federal government sought out his remaining (immediate) relatives and I was one of the family members, that received a check... *"WATCH YOURSELF!"*

Peg Leg

Yep, that was my Dad, he had a *'peg leg,'* I think he had got hit by a car, when he was younger, but he walked with that limp, til the day he died. You could peep him a mile away because of his walk. When he walked, his grandaughter down the aisle, to give her away, for her wedding, he had to take a double step with that one delayed leg, it was quite something to see watching the video play back, (*Thanks Mr. Fleming, our videographer*). Well, I was always close to my Dad; especially as an adult, primarily because *we liked to drink* and now, at 81 years old, I look so much like him, we could be identical twins. When my kids first met him, they would always run, because he'd grab their arm and make them spell words. I would have to yell at them... "*This is your Grandfather, my "Dad,"* (as I affectionately called him), "*just spell the word and he'll let your arm go...*" He'd say, "Daught, spell it...

forgetting the "*er*" altogether at the end, then he'd say spell, "TRUE"... but before you could spell it for him, he'd already say it, "T-R-U-E." It was funny to watch my kids scramble away from him. One time, during the late 1960's, when I had went out of town, as a young *fast* lady, I tried to tell my Dad to lie for me. I was dating a golfer and my children's father, *was shall I say, still in the picture...* Now, mind you, my Dad and my children's father, was the same age *(I know right... go figure... yep, both born in the same month and year, September 22, 1919 and Dad, September 4, 1919).* Well, they got to drinkin'... throwin' em back... Sly asked, "*Where's Pat?*" My Dad replied, "*Oh, she's out of town!*" (Hahaha). Of course, I didn't hear the end of it. But, I fussed so much at my Dad, "*You wasn't supposed to tell him,*" Lo, and behold, I still had a good time, with my friend, driving in the caddy, as the cart was being driven towards the closer holes, what fun... "*WATCH YOURSELF!*"

Family

is

Love

ISTRY CAMP

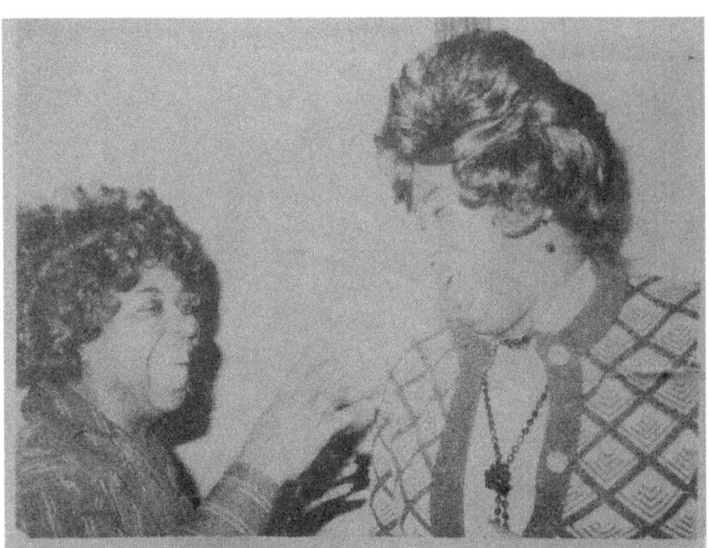

Bun-Bun and Shirley Johnson, at Florence
Speeds party.

PAY ATTENTION!

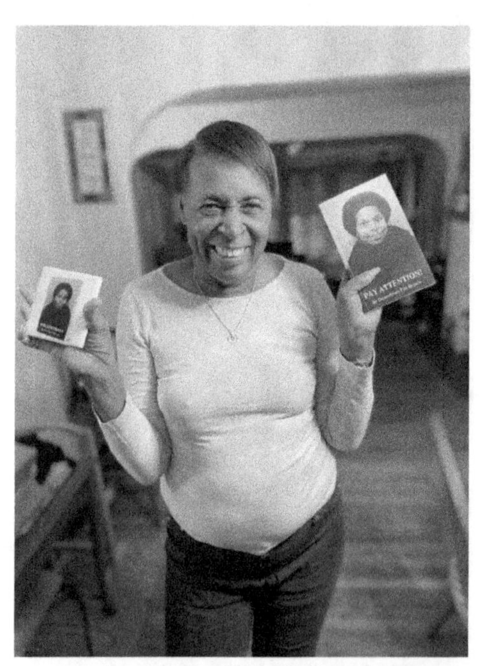

Close Call

In 2013, I became so ill... my children had to rush me to the hospital. Now, mind you, I suffer with *everything*, and even with all of my ailments, *can't nothing slow me down!* My name is... *DOWNTOWN PAT BROWN!* So, if I say I'm sick... I'm really sick, because I know my body. Well, you *know*, that doggone emergency room, is the last place anybody like to go and I be fussing too, all at the *Doctors and Nurses*, mainly because they ask the same questions over and over again, so with my *hypertension*, in full swing, I usually snap, "*It's in my chart!*" And mind you, I always carry my medical cloth book bag, with my medical history, and generally, ask my girls, to reach down in there, in the bag, to answer all their questions. Then, I had to *give* blood, and *get* a blood transfusion. I had lost a lot of blood... I hated to leave my house like that, but my son promised me, that he'd come back and would be sure to bleach and clean up really good. Because, *Lord knows*, if I had the strength, I was going to clean it up, before I went to the hospital; you know, *I can't stand no nasty house.* I wiped up what I could. But I had hit the floor, in pain, and could barely get up. I crawled, on my knees, to my bedroom, to use the phone. (You would think, my frien' who lived downstairs would have come upstairs to check on me, but he didn't, he thought I was cleaning up or something). I *likened to* died that night. But, my baby boy, I call him, "*Main*," came to my rescue and got me to the hospital. So, here I was... had to have all kind of testing and a catscan; tubes and IV's hooked up to me... the works. I mean they were checking for everything... *diabetes, high blood pressure, diverticulitis, my bypasses; the leg and the stint in my heart...* you name it! Then, they think I'm a man, sometimes, because I wear my gray hair very very short, like a thin layer and without my teeth, I look just like my *"Dad."* (The one Doctor apologized for calling me, *'Sir')*. Then, here goes the questions, *"Do you smoke, do you drink, are you sexually active, do this hurt, do that hurt."* In my comedic fashion, of course, I say yes, to everything, including, saying, yes, I'm pregnant now! *Hahaha.* Then I say, *"Yes, it hurt me... you're pressing down on my stomach."* Then, no matter how sick I am, I will sign myself out in a minute, because I don't take the medicine *dey* be *tryna* give me. I yell, *"I don't take that pill!"* And, I put half of 'em down my gown, when they leave out of the room. See, you have to PAY ATTENTION... just because you suffer from something does not mean, you have to take any different medications, just because you're in the hospital. I say, "*NOPE, you can take that nitrate pill on away from me!*" I continue, "*Look, at this paper, that's what I take at home and that's all I'm taking up in here.*" Oh, they listen! They don't have no choice. I don't put nothing under my tongue and never did drugs. They nicknamed me, the '*Silver Fox,*" too. "*WATCH YOURSELF!*"

My Ancestors

Well, to make a long story short, as my *'Close Call'* continues... This time, it was very serious, the Doctor's finally came back *HOURS LATER*, after all the test had come back... I had had an *"Aortic Aneurysm,"* and it blew out my left kidney. *(Told you, I almost died)*. Then, the *Asian* Doctor, was gracious enough, to say, *"Good thing, God gave us two of everything, so if we didn't have the other... we'd still be able to survive."* Then, he went further to say, that it was odd, that I suffered this *"Aortic Aneurysm,"* because the high percentile that it usually happens to is... *'White males.'* I told the Doctor, *"Well, if I go back just 3 generations, 'it's White."* It's in my DNA! So, there you have it. My grandfather's father was *'all White.'* That would be my great grandfather, (who impregnated my Black great grandmother, a laborer in *"the big house,"* and birthed my grandfather. (My *'White'* great great

Grandfather, owned slaves and had three sons, and when he died, his three sons inherited, his slaves, and one of the three son's was Papa's father).). Two years prior, in 2011, my 1st cousin, whose first name is my middle name, '*Elizabeth,*' made sure along with other members of our family, to organize a huge family reunion. We had relatives of *both races* there. We couldn't have been happier, since it had been a long time, (at least over 20 years since we had had a large one and that one was at the JFK Center on Clinton Street); but this reunion covered an entire weekend. Fast forward to 2020, I was proud to say, that at our "*Social Distancing,*" family reunion, held at Dr. MLK, Jr. Park, in September, Papa's 1st cousins were there and not only that, but 7 *living generations* was too! From ages 3 months to 92 years old! *THE SPEED LEGACY NEVER DIES! "WATCH YOURSELF!"*

Get On the Bus

During the Coronavirus shut down

Everything, shut down... But the buses kept running

I was glad, even though I didn't "*have*" to go anywhere, but always do... Even if it ain't nowhere but around the corner to *Mandela's Market*, to play my numbers

Well, the bus driver, told me... once he pulled up to my stop

"Go to the back of the bus." I told him,

"My name NOT Rosa Parks... I sit where I want to sit!"

So, he added, that I wouldn't be able to get back off at the front, because all the passengers had to enter the front of the bus but exit at the back now, due to the Virus...

TELL ME SOMETHING!

Because, I had a moment... I was about to say...

You better... *"WATCH YOURSELF!"*

Pine Grill Jazz Reunion

I had a shelter for the Pine Grill Reunion, *every year*, at MLK Park, for over 20 years and had been going to it for over 30 years (*Rest In Peace, Ms. Agnes Baines, a fixture in the community and the African Cultural Center, who made sure I had a reservation every year... what a beautiful person she was; we lost her two years ago*). Many don't know, but *you know I do*... that the Pine Grill was actually a bar on Jefferson Avenue, (behind *Dexter's Pharmacy* which used to be *Leader's Drug Store*), back in the day. I was only 19 years old, but can remember the Dr. office of *Dr. Lydia Wright*, being in that building too. Matter of fact, that's where I first met my children's father, *Sly*, he was *the Bartender and the Bouncer*... He had that Parliament cigarette cocked behind his ear and drinking scotch, when I first saw him.

(*I got a closet full of scotch now*). *Yea, yea... I dun had my fun... if I don't have no mo'....* Those were the early years... like I told you in my 1st Book, *Pay Attention*, there were bars galore. *One on every other corner!* I wish I could get my hands on an old telephone book, so I could search the yellow pages... that's just how many it was.,,. *Pixie's* was another great hang out spot, just like the Jambouree, Leon's, the Shining Light, Jackson's Corner (at Purdy and E. Ferry Streets), The Governor's Inn, Revelot, Club Savoy, Clover Leaf Bar, Anna's Tavern, the Moon Glow (at Michigan and William Streets), LeClub Etcetera, the Mirage, Foster's, the Zanzibar, Mike's and Luke's Lounge, the Blue Moon and the Little Harlem (which became the Colored Musicians Club, after the Little Harlem burned down, at 145 Broadway Street). But the Pine Grill REUNION, kept getting bigger and bigger and has stood *the test of time.* We even passed it down to the next generation and our children would go too. Children. It ran *the first two Sunday's* in August; filled with tents, food, music, vendors... All my Jazz and Blues people would perform... *RIP Rabbit!* And, if at no other time of the year, you knew (*until the Coronavirus hit*), that you were going to see some of everybody there. But, 2020, if we wanted to see the musicians perform, we would have to watch it online. *Time changes but music remains...* So, for now, one of the best things you can do is... snap your fingers, keep dancing and "*WATCH YOURSELF!*"

Heaven Or Hell Party

Have you ever been to one?
Well, I have!
The way it works is…
You pay $2 coverage charge to go
Upstairs…
to party in Heaven
And $5 to party Downstairs, called *'Hell'*
Downstairs would be filled,
Music jammin'
Dancing, clapping, twirling
all over the place
Getting' down!
That's where all the party people were
but upstairs, it was quiet, chill, partygoers
And at the door, they'd ask…
you wanna go to
Heaven
or
Hell?

Thunderbird

When we ask him,
"What's the word?"
My one and only brother,
Jody Boy,
still responds,
"Thunderbird!
"What's the price?
Thirty twice!"

A Miracle

It had been 22 years, that I had been waiting, to hear those words, "*What's the word... Thunderbird!*" My brother, *Jody Boy*, had wandered off, moved away from the family, without saying goodbye... and for *years*, we didn't have no address *and never ran into him*. The first few years, *in the late '80's*, we would just shrug it off; as he wanted to be left alone and felt that he really hadn't abandoned us altogether. (Although, rumor had it, that he and my other sister, had some '*words*,' and it got heated and he may have heard in earshot, '*I never want to see you again*,' more than likely, they were both intoxicated). But, then years went bye, then decades, and we started asking around, to see if anyone, *family, friend or foe*, had run into him. Our family friend, and Cousin Manny's step-daughter, *Velma,*

(*RIP*), said she had briefly spotted him, getting out of a van, go to the Clinic at the '*Sheehan Memorial Hospital*' (another Landmark on Clinton Street, which formerly used to be just called, '*Emergency Hospital*' gone). We knew for sure that she'd recognize him, because they had dated for the longest, when they were younger. So, after that news, my daughter, CoCo, pleaded, with the family, that the mystery of not seeing my brother, for all of these years, *has gotten out of hand*, and she began her search. She went to the News and Police Station, for help on how to report and how to find, *our missing relative*. For years, I don't think he wanted to be found. But, in our eyes, he was missing out on so much, not to mention, he didn't know that our father passed away and the feuding sister. Everybody was getting older too now and we missed the daylights out of him! CoCo reached out to other relatives, to try and get his social security number, thinking maybe the Social Security Administration could help us, too or at least let us know if he was *dead or alive.* Then, out of the blue, on December 17, 2014, our prayers had been answered. *CoCo* was visiting her Aunt-in-law, (*RIP Aunt Ruthie*) at the nearby nursing home, in her neighborhood, and an Orderly, pushed a man inside, in a wheelchair, with a salt-n-pepper *'signature'* afro, and she screamed to the top of her lungs, "*AHHH, UNCLE JODY BOY!*" My daughter said she went off, threw her coat, flapped her arms, crying tears of joy; (*it'll take her to tell you*)... but she started telling the Staff, *why she was acting in that way,* and they were happy too! Talk about CoCo being in the *right place at the right time*! I am so happy to have my brother back, he's 78 years old now and doing good! I gave him a welcome home celebration, at the nursing home community room, a few weeks after and a lot of the family attended. CoCo also told him that another cousin was in the same facility, one of the Cook's, he even attended the celebration. Jody Boy got used to seeing us all over again and his memory kicked in full gear, and now he's *back like he never left*! As a young man, my brother was always kind and humble, (*well, unless you bothered him, that is*) and very clean (*kept a clean house*) and he always carried a pint of wine in his pocket, his favorite, *M/D 2020*. So wild, that all of those years, he was right under our noses, in a nursing home in Fredonia, NY; not even an hour away from Buffalo, *for 22 years*, and when it closed, their independent residents were relocated to the Buffalo area! Somebody say, "*WATCH YOURSELF*!"

Angel Baby

I should have known my brother,
would be an Angel,
because he was the reason why
I raised my god daughter, Bee Bee.
My daughter CoCo and I
was out roaming the streets,
actually looking for my brother, Jody Boy,
at different houses,
he would disappear *back then too*;
we're talking the late 1960's
so, we went into one
of our family friends houses,
and thought nobody was there,
but then CoCo saw a baby and said,
"Ma, we can't leave the baby
in here all by herself...
Look at her, she's so cute!"
And the rest was history.
Her family became our family,
as I helped to raise
this beautiful baby girl.

Bee Bee is still
so precious to me
til this day!

Don't Worry.... Be Happy

I didn't worry about nothing

I'm carefree...

Always have been

always will be

After having nine children

Plus one God-daughter

make TEN

I didn't have

time to worry

about *this or that*

Cindy Lou

I remember *Cindy Lou*, not feeling well, at *Jody Boy's 'Welcome Home'* Celebration. As a matter of fact, she had already said, (when we called her... with excitement to tell her he'd been found and to let her know that we were having something), that she'd come through, if she felt better. (She would be *M.I.A.* a lot, but mostly at church). *Well, she made it.* It was at least a week before Christmas in 2014, I noticed as everyone was eating, mingling and taking pictures with my brother, that she sat quietly at one of the tables and had gagged a little, and went over to the garbage can to spit it up. We were very concerned, asking her was she alright. She said, *yes.* Then, a few days later, she was in the hospital and while she was in there, I became so stressed, worrying about her and processing my brother's return, I landed in the *same* hospital. We must have worried our family so bad over the next few weeks. They had to go to one floor to see my daughter, (their sister) then... another floor to see me. But, like I told you before, *they not cuttin' all on me, unt-un, cuz I'll sign myself out before I let that happen...* especially when dey came talkin' about, opening up *my* chest... Nope, *no zipper line for me.* But, guess what... it was my oldest daughter, *Cindy Lou,* who got me to work for the Buffalo Public School system. I had already retired and was looking for just a small part time job and she told me that they had a School Bus Aid position opened, (*She worked for the Board and was also a Veteran and Reservist*). Well anyway, they hired me! I was actually at my grandchildren's school, *Buffalo Academy for Visual and Performing Arts*, but didn't have their bus route, so I didn't get to see them. I enjoyed it for the short time that I did it. But, knew it wasn't for me or else I would have to turn into 'Madea' for real. Then, there was 'bowling,' that Cindy Lou got me into... I played on a league with her. Yep! I still have my ball and shoes, (the shoes dun dry rotted now doe, hahahaha). I miss her something terrible, but when I do, I just listen to her favorite record, she sang for the me and the family all the time, at every family gathering, she couldn't get away without singing it, and that was "Dr. Feelgood." She would sing it to perfection like nobody's business, and 'get happy,' at the end of the song. We would cheer so loudly and all I can say now is... before I get too choked up is... "don't fill me with all those pills... cuz, I got me a man named Dr. Feelgood, and he takes care of all my ills"... "WATCH YOURSELF!"

Playing Cards

Can't nobody beat me...
Oh, I was good
I take the cake!
The Gambling Award
of the Year,
Betcha' that!
Betta' jump back jack
Let's play some of my favorites
Tunk
500 Rummy
Gin
Poker (Three Card Molly)
You really lose your money
Black Jack (Head Up)
Then there was dice games
like Crap (Let's roll)
And board games too
Pokeno
Checkers
Bingo
Yahtzee

The Cussin' Club

Y'all don't know
nothin' about these
kind of CLUBS baby…
This party gathering you had
to pay like $3 every time
you say a *curse* word
.50 cents for shit, $1.00 for mf'er
Like that…
But I wasn't a 'cusser'
believe it or not
this party was too funny
Because the members
tried their best not to *cuss*
just so that they wouldn't have
to kick out
so much money.
We took in enough money
to take care of our
casino trips for free!
Back then, trips ran about
$100 round trip and
whoever took care of the pot,

didn't have to pay for food or nothing.
And the bus would leave
from
Mike's Lounge!

Aged Colored Man

Louis Henry Gaffie, my father's grandfather, was born FREE in Louisiana, in the late 1800's. (*Although, at that time, the State of Louisiana was a strong slave state*). He was brought up learning the copper and sugar refining trades; good popular industries back then. He enlisted, during World War II, in the United States Army and served three and a half years. At the time of his discharge, he was stationed at Fort Porter, the U.S. Army base located at 952 Busti Avenue in Buffalo, NY and decided to settle in the Upper Black Rock, side of town, where he lived for thirty-six years and was very well known and was also a worshipper at Holy Angels Church. He was the only *Black man*, at that time, who could *speak fluently in five different languages* and was in high demand as an Interpreter, for the community and City Hall and the first *"Black Catholic" who had ever been buried in Buffalo*; so, I was *born* Catholic and can remember when the Priest used to walk down the street, with their black robe and white cloak around their neck, and a white beaded rosary, stopping to talk with us... We'd say, *"here comes Father so-n-so."* (My Dad, and his cousins went to St. Ann's on Broadway Street and we went to school at St. Mary's School further down Broadway cross Jefferson Avenue). Gaffie was seventy-nine and a half years old, when he passed. His children were Ophelia Cotton, Helen Bradshaw Anderson, Josephine Cook, Maud Cook and Edward T. Gaffie. I was close with both sides of my parents' family and loved my cousins from this tribe, *the Brown's, Cook's, Davis' Josey's, Anderson's, Ford's and Murphy's.* When you meet somebody, ask about their family... their names too... so you won't wind up being 'kissing cousins,' and "*WATCH YOURSELF!*"

The Blues

We would party hardy too...
The whole night through
That's when I was rolling...
I loved the
Jazz and Blues
Still do
Til this day,,,
Shout out to
my cousin
Les Davis
Play it!
I had a huge
record collection
45's... 48's... LP's
And donated majority of them
to Record Theatre
I jammed with the likes of
Joe 'Groove' Madison
Dorothy 'DoDo' Greene
Maurice Sinclaire
Jake the Snake, Slim,

Rick James & the Mary Jane Girls
Count Rabbit, Pappy Martin
James and Lucky Peterson

Gemini

My birthday
lasted all month
I would hit
all the bars up
in my month
June
And they'd say
Whaaat?!
It's your birthday
Give 'er a drink!
and I'd tell people
I'm a Gemini, baby
'Don't let dat twin come out'
Because I'm not
nuttin' to play wit!

While I'm Still On My Feet

As I lay here now, in my bed, relaxin', I reminisce about a lot of *thangs*... How *thangs* are so different now, *yet still the same.* There's so much I remember, *like in '63 when Kennedy was killed and '68 when Martin Luther King, Jr. was assassinated,* and other things, *I choose to forget.* You can't tell people everything, dey takes it the wrong way; use it against you... so some *thangs*, I'll take to the grave with me. But, if I die today or tomorrow, *I have no regrets.* And the one I did have, I had to make *'peace'* with it (since I lost touch with the person). *So that's that.* But, I've lived my life. Didn't think I would still be here, but I am. *Don't sit still! You gotta keep moving.* I get up in the morning *'moving.'* My stomach was bothering me real bad, the other day, and I said, *"unt-un, act right."* Then I got up, got the #8 main Bus and went to the University Plaza to the Dollar Tree and got back into the house; *back like I never left.* If I would have kept laying there, I would have felt so miserable. That's why this last story is called, *"While I'm Still On My Feet."* (And who knows... Book#3). Also, *correction,* for the record, *Papa,* my paternal grandfather, migrated from the South and worked at *Harrison Radiator* but in my 1st book 'Pay Attention,' it was mistakenly written as *Bethlehem Steel,* (which paved the way for many of my people too). I was close with Papa's people too... I loved my great Aunt Emmaline and Cousin Joann and Uncle Ruffin, too! *"Don't let no green grass grow under your feet and if somebody got something to say about it... you just tell them, their grass could be greener too, if they worried about watering their side of the lawn."* Treat peoples right, and don't take from nobody! I haven't had to beg, borrow and steal from nobody. I kid around a lot, like I'm about to pick-pocket 'cha from time to time, but that's all in fun and games. Speaking of fun, back in the day, we had fun just going to the store to get a popsicle on a wooden stick for one cent, made out of ice. Yea, I remember a lot of *thangs*, we had an ice man deliver ice to the house, we had an ice box on the outside, (betcha' can't even find an ice pick nowadays). We would have to chop the ice with an ice pick and when the gas was off, we'd still be able to cook, because we had electric stoves, called 'hot plates.' Look how far I've come from those days, and I'm still on my feet! Anyways, after, I lost my left kidney, in 2013, the doctor's had given me some blood thinners, and I almost bled out; found myself back in the hospital not even two weeks later, as I was telling you earlier, with '*Close Call*,' but my daughters were my saving strength, (*I'm so proud of them*), they were all visiting me together, and then it was time for them to leave, when the recording came over the intercom system, that it was 8pm and time for all visitors to go, as they gathered around my bed, worried about me... turning to leave, I said to them... y'all stick together, don't leave one another and "*WATCH YOURSELF!*"

Accolades

Mayor's Certificate of Merit, (Mayor Anthony Masiello's Office) of Support Services, 1997

Public Service Award, In Recognition of 13 Years, from the Civil Service Employees Asssociation, Local 602, by President Ken Penski, 1984-1997

Buffalo Public School, Bus Aide Awarded, Civil Service Employee, February, 1998

St. Augustine's Senior Companion Program of the United States of America & Child and Family Services, for the invaluable volunteer service to the community, May, 2009

Watch Yourself

Downtown Pat Brown's - Favorite Phrases

Big Things Do Fall
Love Don't Love Nobody
What comes up... Comes out
I ain't funny... I'm for real
Don't nobody owe you nothing
I keeps me some money
Don't sit still... Keep moving
Only the strong survive
Ain't nobody gon' do nothin' for you
The rich get richer... and the poor get
poorer
HOLLA!

www.ingramcontent.com/pod-product-compliance
Lightning Source LLC
Chambersburg PA
CBHW061329120726
48001CB00002B/754